Tarot Card Workbook Journal

Loera Publishing LLC

Table of Contents

Introduction

Tarot cards are so fascinating.

While I have always loved looking at the cards, keeping the meanings straight is sometimes a matter that made me second guess myself.

If one reads cards professionally or just for themselves, how could they learn and remember the cards quickly and easily?

With that thought in mind, I thought, what if I created a workbook that is easy to use, provides a quick reference and allows you to be able to work through a deck by having easy and thought-provoking prompts?

We will go through each card, one by one. Then you will have a series of written exercises to help make each card more real to you, and also to give you some thought provoking questions, often about your own life experiences. There are no right or wrong answers, this is your personal journey.

After we go through each of the cards, we'll cover a variety of spreads for reading tarot cards.

We'll discuss the workbook process a couple pages ahead.

In this book we will be using the Rider-Waite tarot deck as our learning deck.

I hope that you find this workbook helpful and enjoy it as much as we've enjoyed creating it for you.

A Brief History of Tarot Cards

The word tarot comes from the word tarocchi.

Tarocchi is an Italian word whose root—taroch—translates to "foolishness."

The word taroch was used in the 15th century, when trionfi, a 70-card game inspired by the theatrical festivals popular during the Italian Renaissance known as trionfo emerged.

In the 16th century, "the fool" joined this cast of characters, and trionfi game became known as tarocho in Italy and taraux—a term that eventually evolved into tarot—in France.

When trionfi cards emerged in Italy, they were used solely as an entertaining card game.

In 1750, the 62-card Tarocco Bolognese from the 15th-century was among the first decks to be used as a means of fortune-telling.

By the 1780s, people in France were assigning divine meanings to their card decks.

French occultist Jean-Baptiste Alliette is the person known for making the transition from playing card game to fortune telling.

In 1789, Alliette produced a new deck of tarot cards intended solely for fortune telling use. This deck comprises 78 cards organized into two categories: the Major Arcana and the Minor Arcana.

The Major Arcana features 22 cards, each denoting an allegorical figure (The Magician, The High Priestess, The Empress, The Emperor, The Hierophant or Pope, The Hermit, The Hanged Man, The Lovers, The Devil, and The Fool) or personification of an object (The Wheel of Fortune, The Chariot, The Tower, The Star, The Moon, The Sun, and The World) or abstract concept (Strength, Justice, Judgment, Temperance, and Death).

The Major Arcana features four suits (the Suit of Swords, the Suit of Batons, the Suit of Coins, and the Suit of Cups) of 14 cards each. Each suit, in turn, comprises ten numbered cards and four court cards: the King, Queen, Knight, and Jack. These cards are believed to hold the "small secrets" of everyday life.

By the turn of the 20th century, tarot cards—particularly the Tarot of Marseilles—were so entwined with the occult that the Tarot Nouveau, a deck used solely for playing rather than predicting, was created.

How to Use This Workbook

You've received a beautiful set of tarot cards and are eager to learn how to master them and do readings.

Those new to tarot cards are often instructed to keep a tarot journal to help learn the cards.

But how does one start?

You could you draw a random card (daily or weekly) and work your way through the deck.

Keeping track of the cards and their meanings could become a complex and frustrating process.

Trying to decide what to write about and keeping it uniform is another potential problem.

This workbook will guide you, card by card, through the deck in an organized, stress-free manner.

You'll have a resource to refer to as progress.

Remember, this workbook was created for you.

Each person will have different answers to the questions.

Along with learning the meaning of the cards, you will be guided with a series of intriguing questions, to understand the true meaning of each card and associate it with feelings and situations in your own life.

There are no wrong answers. This is truly your own personal journey.

Each card and the associated exercises are on two to four pages.

The Fool 0

Represents all potential possibilities. A blank slate. Trust in the Universe. Taking a risk, being open to anything. Foolishness.

____

____

____

____

How do you feel when you look at the Fool?

Do you see the Fool as positive, negative or neutral? Why? What if the Fool is reversed?

____

____

____

____

Write down a description of the Fool. Try to include

every detail so you really can experience the energy of this card.

____

____

____

____

Make a list of keywords and phrases that help you to understand the Fool.

____

____

____

____

Thinking about your day, how did the Fool manifest itself? This can be about your emotions, memories, events, people – anything.

____

____

____

____

If you could do anything in your life (without having to consider other people, money etc.), what would you do?

____

____

____

____

Describe how it would feel to leap into this new life.

____

____

____

____

The Magician 1

Focus, will power, concentration, control. All the tools available to complete the task in hand. This is the Magician card.

How do you feel when you look at the Magician?

Do you see the Magician as positive, negative or neutral? Why? What if the Magician is reversed?

Write down a description of the Magician.

Try to include every detail so you really can experience the energy of this card.

Make a list of keywords and phrases that help you to understand the Magician.

Thinking about your day, how did the Magician manifest itself? This manifestation can be about your emotions, memories, events, people – anything.

What could you start right now?

What would need to be put into place to make it happen?

The High Priestess 2

Intuition, silence, stillness. Keeper of secrets and mystery. Maidenhood. Spiritual contemplation.

How do you feel when you look at the High Priestess?

Do you see the High Priestess as positive, negative or neutral? Why? What if the High Priestess is reversed?

Write down a description of the High Priestess. Try to include every detail so you really can experience the energy of this card.

____

____

____

____

Make a list of keywords and phrases that help you to understand the High Priestess.

____

____

____

Thinking about your day, how did the High Priestess manifest itself? This can be about your emotions, memories, events, people – anything.

____

____

____

Do you use your intuition to make decisions?

____

____

____

Remember a past example and write it down.

____

____

____

Was it a good choice?

____

____

____

____

Describe how your intuition manifests in your body.

____

____

____

____

The Empress 3

Abundance, nurturing, motherhood. Growth, fruition. Cultivation.

How do you feel when you look at the Empress?

____

____

____

____

Do you see the Empress as positive, negative or neutral? Why? What if the Empress is reversed?

____

____

____

____

Write down a description of the Empress. Try to include every detail so you really can experience the energy of this card.

____

____

Make a list of keywords and phrases that help you to understand the Empress.

Thinking about your day, how did the Empress manifest itself? This can be about your emotions, memories, events, people – anything.

Who and what do you appreciate in your life?

Write down specifics regarding who and what you appreciate.

The Emperor 4

Structure, power. Masculinity, fatherhood. Rule setter. Business success.

How do you feel when you look at the Emperor?

____

____

____

____

Do you see the Emperor as positive, negative or neutral? Why?

____

____

____

____

What if the Emperor is reversed?

____

____

____

____

Write down a description of the Emperor. Try to include every detail so you really can experience the energy of this card.

Make a list of keywords and phrases that help you to understand the Emperor.

Thinking about your day, how did the Emperor manifest itself? This can be about your emotions, memories, events, people – anything.

Do you have a personal code of conduct?

What self-imposed rules would you never break?

The Hierophant 5

Spiritual guide, mentor, religion, faith. Established institution.

How do you feel when you look at the Hierophant?

____

____

____

____

Do you see the Hierophant as positive, negative or neutral? Why?

____

____

____

____

What if the Hierophant is reversed?

____

____

____

A detailed description in your own words helps you to really feel the energy of a card. Write down a description of the Hierophant. Try to include every detail.

____

____

____

Make a list of keywords and phrases that help you to understand the Hierophant.

____

____

____

Thinking about your day, how did the Hierophant manifest itself? This can be about your emotions, memories, events, people – anything.

____

____

____

Do you inspire others?

____

____

Who inspires you?

____

____

Who has had the most positive influence in your life?

____

____

____

How?

____

____

____

The Lovers 6

Love, sex, relationships. Choices, life-changing decisions.

How do you feel when you look at the Lovers?

Do you see the Lovers as positive, negative or neutral? Why?

What if the Lovers is reversed?

A detailed description in your own words helps you to really feel the energy of a card. Write down a description of the Lovers. Try to include every detail.

____

____

____

____

Make a list of keywords and phrases that help you to understand the Lovers.

____

____

____

____

Thinking about your day, how did the Lovers manifest itself? This can be about your emotions, memories, events, people – anything.

____

____

____

____

It is said that you can't love someone else unless you can love yourself first.

____

____

____

____

Do you think this is true?

____

____

____

____

Why?

____

____

____

The Chariot 7

Self-discipline, determination, goal seeking. Negotiation, mediation. Gathering resources and driving oneself forward. Travel, journey.

How do you feel when you look at the Chariot?

Do you see the Chariot as positive, negative or neutral? Why?

What if the Chariot is reversed?

____

____

____

A detailed description in your own words helps you to really feel the energy of a card.
Write down a description of the Chariot. Try to include every detail.

____

____

____

Make a list of keywords and phrases that help you to understand the Chariot.

____

____

____

Thinking about your day, how did the Chariot manifest itself? This can be about your
emotions, memories, events, people – anything.

____

____

____

Do you control your thoughts and emotions, or do they control you?

____

____

____

Have you ever tried to keep your thoughts focused on only one thing or task?

____

____

____

How did it work out?

____

____

____

____

Strength 8

Inner strength, persuasion, gentleness, trust, tactfulness, diplomacy, patience. Kindness to animals, children and those in need.

How do you feel when you look at Strength?

Do you see Strength as positive, negative or neutral? Why?

What if the Strength card is reversed?

A detailed description in your own words helps you to really feel the energy of a card. Write down a description of Strength. Try to include every detail.

Make a list of keywords and phrases that help you to understand Strength.

Think about your day, how did Strength manifest itself? This can be about your emotions, memories, events, people – anything.

When did you discover you had inner reserves of strength?

Did you surprise yourself by how well you coped? Why or why not?

The Hermit 9

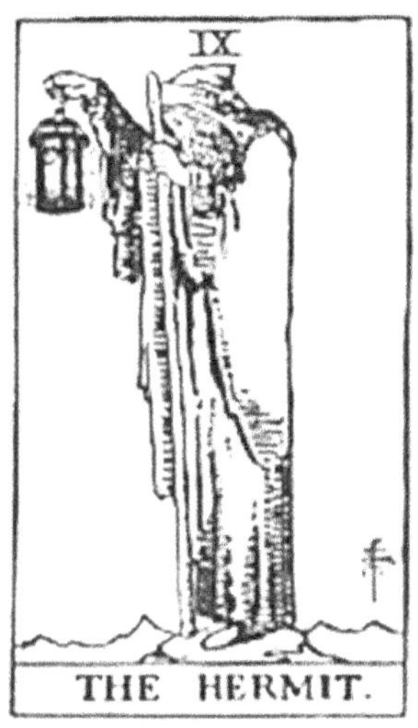

Solitude, introspection, self-knowledge, study, withdrawal from relationships. Time to pause and think.

____

____

____

____

How do you feel when you look at the Hermit?

____

____

____

____

Do you see the Hermit as positive, negative or neutral? Why? What if the Hermit is reversed?

____

____

____

A detailed description in your own words helps you to really feel the energy of a card. Write down a description of the Hermit. Try to include every detail.

Make a list of keywords and phrases that help you to understand the Hermit.

Thinking about your day, how did the Hermit manifest itself? This can be about your emotions, memories, events, people – anything.

Do you enjoy solitude?   Why or why not?

Are you comfortable when left alone with your thoughts?

Do you continually seek company?

Why?

The Wheel of Fortune 10

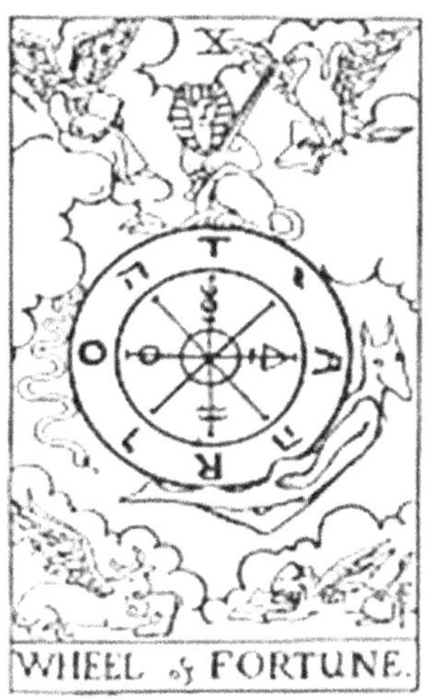

Anything could happen. Changes, cycles, chance. Combined with other cards: good or bad fortune.

How do you feel when you look at the Wheel of Fortune?

Do you see the Wheel of Fortune as positive, negative or neutral? Why? What if the Wheel of Fortune is reversed?

A detailed description in your own words helps you to really feel the energy of a card. Write down a description of the Wheel of Fortune. Try to include every detail.

____

____

____

____

Make a list of keywords and phrases that help you to understand the Wheel of Fortune.

____

____

____

____

Thinking about your day, how did the Wheel of Fortune manifest itself? This can be about your emotions, memories, events, people – anything.

____

____

____

____

Do you spin your own wheel?

____

____

____

What do you do when life gets out of control?

(Hint: Things are more controllable when you are at the center of the wheel).

____

____

____

____

Do we control our destiny? Why or why not?

____

____

____

Justice 11

Legal issue, court case, settlement, retribution, divorce finalizes, property conveyancing. Career connected to law or contracts. Balance. Fairness.

How do you feel when you look at Justice?

Do you see Justice as positive, negative or neutral? Why?

What if Justice is reversed?

A detailed description in your own words helps you to really feel the energy of a card. Write down a description of Justice. Try to include every detail.

Make a list of keywords and phrases that help you to understand Justice.

Thinking about your day, how did Justice manifest itself? This can be about your emotions, memories, events, people – anything.

Do you think justice is about retribution, punishment or to balance the scale of fairness?

What does the concept of justice mean to you personally?

The Hanged Man 12

Enforced inactivity. No apparent progression. Stagnation. Waiting time. Forced to look at the situation from another perspective. Acceptance.

Letting go.

How do you feel when you look at the Hanged Man?

Do you see the Hanged Man as positive, negative or neutral? Why?

What if the Hanged Man is reversed?

____

____

____

A detailed description in your own words helps you to really feel the energy of a card.
Write down a description of the Hanged Man. Try to include every detail.

____

____

____

Make a list of keywords and phrases that help you to understand the Hanged Man.

____

____

____

Thinking about your day, how did the Hanged Man manifest itself? This can be about
your emotions, memories, events, people – anything.

____

____

____

Have you ever been forced to change your beliefs?

____

____

____

How did that feel?

____

____

____

Can you remember a time when giving up felt like relief?

____

____

____

Death 13

Death and rebirth. An important stage of life is ending – career, job, relationship. Retirement. Release, transformation. Life cycles.

How do you feel when you look at the Death card?

Do you see Death as positive, negative or neutral? Why?

What if Death is reversed?

A detailed description in your own words helps you to really feel the energy of a card. Write down a description of Death. Try to include every detail.

Make a list of keywords and phrases that help you to understand Death.

Thinking about your day, how did Death manifest itself? This can be about your emotions, memories, events, people – anything.

Does the thought of dying scare you?

Why?

Do you think you can come to terms with your death?

Imagine you just died - write down a conversation you might have with Death.

Temperance 14

Harmony, healing, integration, moderation. Thoughtfulness and caution. Good chemistry, balance. Conservation and care of the environment.

How do you feel when you look at Temperance?

Do you see Temperance as positive, negative or neutral? Why?

What if Temperance is reversed?

____

____

____

____

A detailed description in your own words helps you to really feel the energy of a card.
Write down a description of Temperance. Try to include every detail.

____

____

____

____

Make a list of keywords and phrases that help you to understand Temperance.

____

____

____

____

Thinking about your day, how did Temperance manifest itself? This can be about your
emotions, memories, events, people – anything.

____

____

____

____

Describe what it feels like to be out of balance in mind, body and spirit.

____

____

____

____

How do you regain your equilibrium?

____

____

____

The Devil 15

Addiction, enslavement, holding on to that which does not serve you. Stuck in a bad relationship or other situation. Sometimes, "Being a devil" as in, having fun, enjoying sweets, being devilish.

How do you feel when you look at the Devil?

Do you see the Devil as positive, negative or neutral? Why? What if the Devil is reversed?

A detailed description in your own words helps you to really feel the energy of a card. Write down a description of the Devil. Try to include every detail.

Make a list of keywords and phrases that help you to understand the Devil.

Thinking about your day, how did the Devil manifest itself? This can be about your emotions, memories, events, people – anything.

Have you ever felt powerless in a situation?

How did you finally break through the feeling of powerless?

Do you believe that love can conquer evil?

How so?

The Tower 16

Perceived catastrophe. Clear out. Energetic transformation. Loss, accident, 'end of the world'. Removal of obstacles. Starting over.

___

How do you feel when you look at the Tower?

___

Do you see the Tower as positive, negative or neutral? Why?

___

What if the Tower is reversed?

___

A detailed description in your own words helps you to really feel the energy of a card. Write down a description of the Tower. Try to include every detail.

Make a list of keywords and phrases that help you to understand the Tower.

Thinking about your day, how did the Tower manifest itself? This can be about your emotions, memories, events, people – anything.

What would be your absolute worse nightmare coming true?

Would you have the determination to rebuild your life?

Has it already happened and if so, did you rebuild? Write down details.

The Star 17

Hope, peace, love. Triumph of good over bad. Looking forward; moving on. Blessings, healing.

How do you feel when you look at the Star?

Do you see the Star as positive, negative or neutral? Why? What if the Star is reversed?

A detailed description in your own words helps you to really feel the energy of a card. Write down a description of the Star. Try to include every detail.

Make a list of keywords and phrases that help you to understand the Star.

Thinking about your day, how did the Star manifest itself? This can be about your emotions, memories, events, people – anything.

What blessings do you hold dear in your life?

Name some of those blessings.

The Moon 18

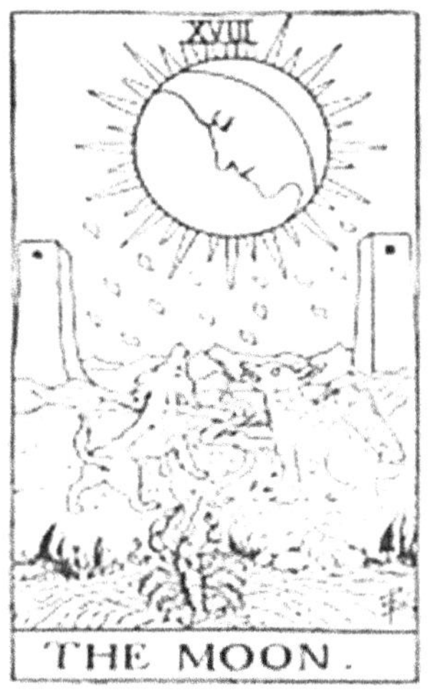

Confusion, distraction, deceptive circumstances, losing one's way, distorted perception, poor mental health. Need of intuition to get back on track. Cycles, currents, tides.

____

____

____

How do you feel when you look at the Moon?

____

____

Do you see the Moon as positive, negative or neutral? Why?

____

____

____

What if the Moon is reversed?

____

____

A detailed description in your own words helps you to really feel the energy of a card. Write down a description of the Moon. Try to include every detail.

Make a list of keywords and phrases that help you to understand the Moon.

Thinking about your day, how did the Moon manifest itself? This can be about your emotions, memories, events, people – anything.

Did you ever step into a situation that appeared perfect for you but later proved to be so very wrong?

How did you become aware of the error?

How did you correct your path or are you correcting it now?

If not you, do you know someone that this happened to? How did they handle the matter?

The Sun 19

Growth, happiness, mindfulness. All aspects of life improve. Making the most of the good times. Living in the moment.

How do you feel when you look at the Sun?

Do you see the Sun as positive, negative or neutral? Why?

What if the Sun is reversed?

____

____

____

A detailed description in your own words helps you to really feel the energy of a card.
Write down a description of the Sun. Try to include every detail.

____

____

____

Make a list of keywords and phrases that help you to understand the Sun.

____

____

____

Thinking about your day, how did the Sun manifest itself? This can be about your
emotions, memories, events, people – anything.

____

____

____

What makes you feel full of sunshine and happiness?

____

____

____

What's your favorite thing to do when the sun is shining?

____

____

____

What does happiness look like? Does it have a taste or smell?

____

____

Judgement 20

A call to action; something you must do. A wake-up call. Be accountable; responsible. Karma. Change of career or lifestyle.

____

____

____

How do you feel when you look at Judgement?

____

____

____

Do you see the Judgement card as positive, negative or neutral? Why?

____

____

____

What if Judgement is reversed?

____

____

A detailed description in your own words helps you to really feel the energy of a card. Write down a description of Judgement. Try to include every detail.

Make a list of keywords and phrases that help you to understand Judgement.

Thinking about your day, how did Judgement manifest itself? This can be about your emotions, memories, events, people – anything.

Have you ever had an epiphany?

(Epiphany definition: A moment when you suddenly feel that you understand, or suddenly become conscious of something)

Have you ever felt compelled to do something out of character?

Imagine that tomorrow is the last day of your life – how would you spend it? Who would you call or see? What would you say or do?

The World 21

Right where you need to be. Completion, fulfilment, attainment. End of a life cycle. Pause, transition, waiting.

How do you feel when you look at the World?

Do you see the World as positive, negative or neutral? Why?

What if the World is reversed?

____

____

____

____

A detailed description in your own words helps you to really feel the energy of a card. Write down a description of the World. Try to include every detail.

____

____

____

____

Make a list of keywords and phrases that help you to understand the World.

____

____

____

____

Thinking about your day, how did the World manifest itself? This can be about your emotions, memories, events, people – anything.

____

____

____

____

Have you experienced distinct stages throughout your life?

____

____

____

____

Recall and describe the end of any of these stages and how you moved onto the next one.

____

____

____

Ace of Wands

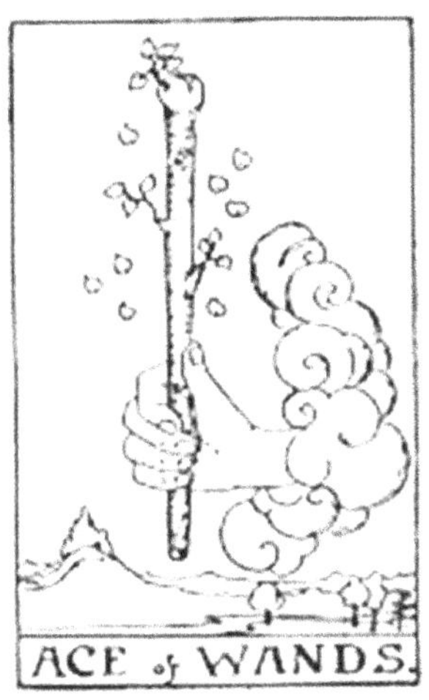

New initiatives, ideas or inspiration. Optimism, feeling in control, ready for anything. Change of lifestyle or new personal image. New business or enterprise. High energy levels. Birth of a baby.

How do you feel when you look at the Ace of Wands?

Do you see the Ace of Wands as positive, negative or neutral? Why? What if the Ace of Wands is reversed?

A detailed description in your own words helps you to really feel the energy of a card. Write down a description of the Ace of Wands. Try to include every detail.

Make a list of keywords and phrases that help you to understand the Ace of Wands.

Thinking about your day, how did the Ace of Wands manifest itself? This can be about your emotions, memories, events, people – anything.

How do you feel when inspiration strikes?

Can you remember when a new idea came to you and your optimism felt boundless?

What happened?

Did you bring it to fruition?

Two of Wands

Planning stage. Minor decisions must be made, details to be ironed out. Possible frustration. Apparent lack of progress.

How do you feel when you look at the Two of Wands?

Do you see the Two of Wands as positive, negative or neutral? Why?

What if the Two of Wands is reversed?

A detailed description in your own words helps you to really feel the energy of a card. Write down a description of the Two of Wands. Try to include every detail.

ke a list of keywords and phrases that help you to understand the Two of Wands.

Thinking about your day, how did the Two of Wands manifest itself? This can be about your emotions, memories, events, people – anything.

Do you enjoy the planning stage of a project?

Do you feel frustrated when you know where you want to get to but are held up by small obstacles?

How do you deal with obstacles?

Three of Wands

Success is on the horizon. Hard work is beginning to pay off. Positive forward momentum. Anticipation of good things to come.

How do you feel when you look at the Three of Wands?

Do you see the Three of Wands as positive, negative or neutral? Why? What if the Three of Wands is reversed?

A detailed description in your own words helps you to really feel the energy of a card. Write down a description of the Three of Wands. Try to include every detail.

Make a list of keywords and phrases that help you to understand the Three of Wands.

Thinking about your day, how did the Three of Wands manifest itself? This can be about your emotions, memories, events, people – anything.

Do you enjoy having everything organized aka, all your ducks in a row?

Are you the sort of person who expects the best outcome when doing something?

Does failure make you want to give up or does it make you more determined?

Four of Wands

Completion of work, consolidation, fruition. A temporary resting period. New home, marriage.

How do you feel when you look at the Four of Wands?

Do you see the Four of Wands as positive, negative or neutral? Why? What if the Four of Wands is reversed?

A detailed description in your own words helps you to really feel the energy of a card.

Write down a description of the Four of Wands. Try to include every detail.

____

____

____

Make a list of keywords and phrases that help you to understand the Four of Wands.

____

____

____

Thinking about your day, how did the Four of Wands manifest itself? This can be about your emotions, memories, events, people – anything.

____

____

____

The satisfaction of a job well done is most always a great feeling. When was the last time you felt this sense of accomplishment?

____

____

____

Describe the details of the project and why you felt so good after finishing.

____

____

____

Is there anything, however small, you can complete today to enable you to achieve that sense of accomplishment satisfaction?

____

____

____

If so, take the time to do it and write down how you felt afterwards.

____

____

____

Five of Wands

Arguments, disputes, squabbling that could escalate if not checked. Skirmishes, nit-picking, bullying.

How do you feel when you look at the Five of Wands?

Do you see the Five of Wands as positive, negative or neutral? Why?

What if the Five of Wands is reversed?

A detailed description in your own words helps you to really feel the energy of a card. Write down a description of the Five of Wands. Try to include every detail.

Make a list of keywords and phrases that help you to understand the Five of Wands.

Thinking about your day, how did the Five of Wands manifest itself? This can be about your emotions, memories, events, people – anything.

Do you shy away from a confrontation, or do you look for it?

How do you feel afterward a confrontation?

Would you rather be right or happy?

Why?

Six of Wands

Recognition and praise. Good news.

How do you feel when you look at the Six of Wands?

Do you see the Six of Wands as positive, negative or neutral? Why?

What if the Six of Wands is reversed?

____

____

____

____

A detailed description in your own words helps you to really feel the energy of a card. Write down a description of the Six of Wands. Try to include every detail.

____

____

____

____

Make a list of keywords and phrases that help you to understand the Six of Wands.

____

____

____

____

Thinking about your day, how did the Six of Wands manifest itself? This can be about your emotions, memories, events, people – anything.

____

____

____

____

Take a moment to recognize your small (and/or large) successes today.

____

____

____

____

Didn't have any? Pay attention tomorrow and be ready to congratulate yourself.

____

____

____

Seven of Wands

Challenges, pressure, questioning of your beliefs, opinions, position and policies. Defending your point of view. Prevailing against the odds.

____

____

____

How do you feel when you look at the Seven of Wands?

____

____

____

Do you see the Seven of Wands as positive, negative or neutral? Why? What if the Seven of Wands is reversed?

____

____

____

A detailcd description in your own words helps you to really feel the energy of a card. Write down a description of the Seven of Wands. Try to include every detail.

Make a list of keywords and phrases that help you to understand the Seven of Wands.

Thinking about your day, how did the Seven of Wands manifest itself? This can be about your emotions, memories, events, people – anything.

Have you ever been put under pressure from friends, family or employer?

Do you know when to hold your ground and when to concede?

Describe a time when you held your ground.

Were you pleased with the results?

Why?

Eight of Wands

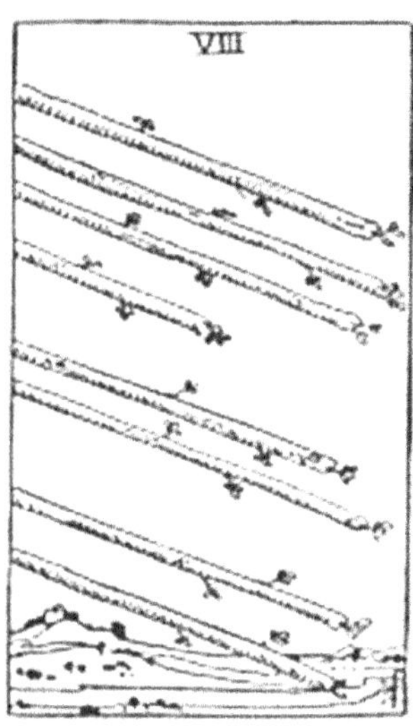

Fast moving changes. Driving forward. Get organised! Group projects. Travel. Pregnancy.

How do you feel when you look at the Eight of Wands?

Do you see the Eight of Wands as positive, negative or neutral? Why?

What if the Eight of Wands is reversed?

A detailed description in your own words helps you to really feel the energy of a card. Write down a description of the Eight of Wands. Try to include every detail.

Make a list of keywords and phrases that help you to understand the Eight of Wands.

Thinking about your day, how did the Eight of Wands manifest itself? This can be about your emotions, memories, events, people – anything.

Think about a time when you had to respond to an emergency. Were you calm and organized or was there a sense of panic?

Would you consider co-ordinating and/or leading a group project?

How do you think people would respond to you?

Nine of Wands

Setback, momentary defeat or lack of energy. Perseverance in the face of adversity. Determination. Regrouping.

How do you feel when you look at the Nine of Wands?

Do you see the Nine of Wands as positive, negative or neutral? Why?

What if the Nine of Wands is reversed?

A detailed description in your own words helps you to really feel the energy of a card. Write down a description of the Nine of Wands. Try to include every detail.

Make a list of keywords and phrases that help you to understand the Nine of Wands.

Thinking about your day, how did the Nine of Wands manifest itself? This can be about your emotions, memories, events, people – anything.

Have you ever felt like giving up but got through something due to sheer determination?

Describe the situation and the outcome.

Have you ever given up and then later, wished you hadn't?

Do you feel you are stubborn?

Why?

Is it a good thing or bad thing (if you are stubborn or not)?

Why?

Ten of Wands

Overburdened. Too many responsibilities. Debt. Struggle. Life is one long uphill plod.

How do you feel when you look at the Ten of Wands?

Do you see the Ten of Wands as positive, negative or neutral? Why?

What if the Ten of Wands is reversed?

A detailed description in your own words helps you to really feel the energy of a card. Write down a description of the Ten of Wands. Try to include every detail.

Make a list of keywords and phrases that help you to understand the Ten of Wands.

Thinking about your day, how did the Ten of Wands manifest itself? This can be about your emotions, memories, events, people – anything.

Do you have a preferred way to handle feelings of being overwhelmed?

Are you able to say no to someone without feeling guilty?

Have you been able to keep yourself free of unnecessary work or burdens by being able to say no?

Page of Wands

Explorer of possibilities. Full of ideas and enthusiasm. On the cusp of an adventure. Young energetic person. Important message is imminent.

How do you feel when you look at the Page of Wands?

Do you see the Page of Wands as positive, negative or neutral? Why?

What if the Page of Wands is reversed?

A detailed description in your own words helps you to really feel the energy of a card. Write down a description of the Page of Wands. Try to include every detail.

Make a list of keywords and phrases that help you to understand the Page of Wands.

Thinking about your day, how did the Page of Wands manifest itself? This can be about your emotions, memories, events, people – anything.

What has been your greatest adventure?

Do you think we ever realize our full potential?

Why or why not?

Do you like having something to look forward to? Why or why not?

Knight of Wands

Ambitious, brave, passionate, hasty. Eagerness. Full of energy. Transition. Unreliable, temperamental.

____

____

____

How do you feel when you look at the Knight of Wands?

____

____

____

Do you see the Knight of Wands as positive, negative or neutral? Why?

____

____

____

What if the Knight of Wands is reversed?

A detailed description in your own words helps you to really feel the energy of a card. Write down a description of the Knight of Wands. Try to include every detail.

Make a list of keywords and phrases that help you to understand the Knight of Wands.

Thinking about your day, how did the Knight of Wands manifest itself? This can be about your emotions, memories, events, people – anything.

Have you ever felt as though you wanted to do something with all your soul and suddenly, later, you lost interest?

Did you ever want something passionately and when you got it, it meant nothing?

Do you know a Knight of Wands?

Queen of Wands

Warm, ambitious, fun, flirty, cheerful. Extrovert. Sexually passionate. Disorganised, promiscuous.

How do you feel when you look at the Queen of Wands?

Do you see the Queen of Wands as positive, negative or neutral? Why?

What if the Queen of Wands is reversed?

A detailed description in your own words helps you to really feel the energy of a card. Write down a description of the Queen of Wands. Try to include every detail.

Make a list of keywords and phrases that help you to understand the Queen of Wands.

Thinking about your day, how did the Queen of Wands manifest itself? This can be about your emotions, memories, events, people – anything.

Do you know a Queen of Wands?

Are you a Queen of Wands?

Would you like to be a Queen of Wands?

What do you like best about her?

What do you dislike about her?

King of Wands

Inspirational, optimistic, successful. Passionate. Strong leader. Rule breaker. Hot tempered, shouty and irritable; bad moods pass quickly.

How do you feel when you look at the King of Wands?

Do you see the King of Wands as positive, negative or neutral? Why? What if the King of Wands is reversed?

A detailed description in your own words helps you to really feel the energy of a card. Write down a description of the King of Wands. Try to include every detail.

Make a list of keywords and phrases that help you to understand the King of Wands.

Thinking about your day, how did the King of Wands manifest itself? This can be about your emotions, memories, events, people – anything.

Do you know a King of Wands?

Are you a King of Wands?

What do you like least/best about the King of Wands character?

Ace of Cups

New friendship, love. Emotional happiness and fulfilment. Strengthening or renewal of an important relationship. Conception.

How do you feel when you look at the Ace of Cups?

Do you see the Ace of Cups as positive, negative or neutral? Why?

What if the Ace of Cups is reversed?

A detailed description in your own words helps you to really feel the energy of a card. Write down a description of the Ace of Cups. Try to include every detail.

Make a list of keywords and phrases that help you to understand the Ace of Cups.

Thinking about your day, how did the Ace of Cups manifest itself? This can be about your emotions, memories, events, people – anything.

Have you ever looked at someone and fell completely head over heels in love?

Describe the feeling.

Did you ever meet someone and know that they would become a friend for life?

Two of Cups

Mutual attraction. Deepening friendship Forging an emotional bond. Knowing true love.

How do you feel when you look at the Two of Cups?

Do you see the Two of Cups as positive, negative or neutral? Why?

What if the Two of Cups is reversed?

A detailed description in your own words helps you to really feel the energy of a card. Write down a description of the Two of Cups. Try to include every detail.

Make a list of keywords and phrases that help you to understand the Two of Cups.

Thinking about your day, how did the Two of Cups manifest itself? This can be about your emotions, memories, events, people – anything.

If you had to choose between love and friendship, which would it be?

Why?

Are relationships better after the initial falling-in-love has passed?

Why?

Three of Cups

Family and friends celebration. Growing circle of friends. Cementing emotional bonds. Losing inhibitions.

____

____

____

How do you feel when you look at the Three of Cups?

____

____

____

Do you see the Three of Cups as positive, negative or neutral? Why?

____

____

____

What if the Three of Cups is reversed?

____

____

A detailed description in your own words helps you to really feel the energy of a card. Write down a description of the Three of Cups. Try to include every detail.

Make a list of keywords and phrases that help you to understand the Three of Cups.

Thinking about your day, how did the Three of Cups manifest itself? This can be about your emotions, memories, events, people – anything.

Do you enjoy getting together with friends and family? Or do you prefer not attending get togethers or parties if possible? Why?

How much do you share with your friends?

Do they know everything about you?

Why or why not?

Four of Cups

Withdrawn. Low-level depression – usually temporary. Unseeing of opportunities. Lack of enthusiasm. Detachment. Alternatively: emotional stability; a levelling out, ignoring temptation.

____

____

____

____

How do you feel when you look at the Four of Cups?

____

____

____

____

Do you see the Four of Cups as positive, negative or neutral? Why?

____

____

____

What if the Four of Cups is reversed?

____

____

____

A detailed description in your own words helps you to really feel the energy of a card. Write down a description of the Four of Cups. Try to include every detail.

____

____

____

____

Make a list of keywords and phrases that help you to understand the Four of Cups.

____

____

____

____

Thinking about your day, how did the Four of Cups manifest itself? This can be about your emotions, memories, events, people – anything.

____

____

____

____

Do you see temporary withdrawal as a necessity to regain emotional balance?

____

____

____

____

If you notice that someone you love seems depressed or withdrawn, do you try to cheer them up or do you feel they should be left alone?

____

____

____

Five of Cups

Grief, loss, despair. Deep, long-lasting depression. All is not lost – there is always a way through.

How do you feel when you look at the Five of Cups?

Do you see the Five of Cups as positive, negative or neutral? Why?

What if the Five of Cups is reversed?

A detailed description in your own words helps you to really feel the energy of a card. Write down a description of the Five of Cups. Try to include every detail.

Make a list of keywords and phrases that help you to understand the Five of Cups.

Thinking about your day, how did the Five of Cups manifest itself? This can be about your emotions, memories, events, people – anything.

Have you experienced grief first-hand?

Who or what comforted you?

How did you manage to move through it?

Have you witnessed deep emotional pain in another person?

Could you try to describe that pain as if it were you experiencing it?

Six of Cups

Emotional recovery. Renewing friendships and acquaintances. Nostalgia, childhood, children. Playfulness. Revisiting places where you were happiest. Life feels lighter.

How do you feel when you look at the Six of Cups?

Do you see the Six of Cups as positive, negative or neutral? Why?

What if the Six of Cups is reversed?

A detailed description in your own words helps you to really feel the energy of a card. Write down a description of the Six of Cups. Try to include every detail.

Make a list of keywords and phrases that help you to understand the Six of Cups.

Thinking about your day, how did the Six of Cups manifest itself? This can be about your emotions, memories, events, people – anything.

Who do you miss from your past?

What is your favorite memory of them?

Was your childhood good in your opinion or were you glad to move into adulthood? Why?

Seven of Cups

Decision overload. Daydreaming about possibilities instead of doing something about them. Emotional overwhelm. Feeling that you are at an emotional crossroads.

____

____

____

How do you feel when you look at the Seven of Cups?

____

____

____

Do you see the Seven of Cups as positive, negative or neutral? Why? What if the Seven of Cups is reversed?

____

____

____

A detailed description in your own words helps you to really feel the energy of a card. Write down a description of the Seven of Cups. Try to include every detail.

Make a list of keywords and phrases that help you to understand the Seven of Cups.

Thinking about your day, how did the Seven of Cups manifest itself? This can be about your emotions, memories, events, people – anything.

When it comes to decision making – how do you act – are you quick, spontaneous or slow?

Do you have regrets over any past decisions that ended up being life changing choices?

Why or why not?

Eight of Cups

An emotional decision has been made. Turning away from a situation. Taking a more difficult path. Leaving love (or pain) behind.

____

____

____

How do you feel when you look at the Eight of Cups?

____

____

____

Do you see the Eight of Cups as positive, negative or neutral? Why?

____

____

____

What if the Eight of Cups is reversed?

____

A detailed description in your own words helps you to really feel the energy of a card. Write down a description of the Eight of Cups. Try to include every detail.

Make a list of keywords and phrases that help you to understand the Eight of Cups.

Thinking about your day, how did the Eight of Cups manifest itself? This can be about your emotions, memories, events, people – anything.

Imagine having to pack up just what you can carry and walk out the door, leaving everyone and everything behind.

How would you feel? Where would you go and why?

Nine of Cups

Contentment. Emotional fulfilment. Well-being. Pleasure. Ease. A happy life.

How do you feel when you look at the Nine of Cups?

Do you see the Nine of Cups as positive, negative or neutral? Why? What if the Nine of Cups is reversed?

A detailed description in your own words helps you to really feel the energy of a card. Write down a description of the Nine of Cups. Try to include every detail.

Make a list of keywords and phrases that help you to understand the Nine of Cups.

Thinking about your day, how did the Nine of Cups manifest itself? This can be about your emotions, memories, events, people – anything.

Right now, in this very moment (not last minute, or next minute), all is well – do you agree?

Describe the utter perfection of your life in this very moment.

Ten of Cups

Family. Love. A happy marriage or partnership. A journey ended. Home. Emotional security.

____

____

____

How do you feel when you look at the Ten of Cups?

____

____

____

Do you see the Ten of Cups as positive, negative or neutral? Why?

____

____

____

What if the Ten of Cups is reversed?

____

____

A detailed description in your own words helps you to really feel the energy of a card. Write down a description of the Ten of Cups. Try to include every detail.

Make a list of keywords and phrases that help you to understand the Ten of Cups.

Thinking about your day, how did the Ten of Cups manifest itself? This can be about your emotions, memories, events, people – anything.

If you live alone, is it possible to be a happy family unit?

Is your family close-knit or do you appreciate the distance between you and them?

What does the word 'home' mean to you?

Page of Cups

Explorer of human emotion. Creative, artistic. Healer. A young child or baby. A message delivered in person

How do you feel when you look at the Page of Cups?

Do you see the Page of Cups as positive, negative or neutral? Why?

What if the Page of Cups is reversed?

A detailed description in your own words helps you to really feel the energy of a card. Write down a description of the Page of Cups. Try to include every detail.

Make a list of keywords and phrases that help you to understand the Page of Cups.

Thinking about your day, how did the Page of Cups manifest itself? This can be about your emotions, memories, events, people – anything.

Are you willing to explore the whole range of emotions from grief to joy?

Can you allow yourself to really feel deep emotion, rather than just reacting to external stimulus?

What was the worst news someone told you?

What was the best news someone told you?

Can you perform one creative action today? What is it? How do you feel after finishing the action?

Knight of Cups

Romance, lover, bringer of gifts. A romantic fling. Sharing of feelings. Can be shallow – in love with falling in love.

How do you feel when you look at the Knight of Cups?

Do you see the Knight of Cups as positive, negative or neutral? Why?

What if the Knight of Cups is reversed?

A detailed description in your own words helps you to really feel the energy of a card. Write down a description of the Knight of Cups. Try to include every detail.

Make a list of keywords and phrases that help you to understand the Knight of Cups.

Thinking about your day, how did the Knight of Cups manifest itself? This can be about your emotions, memories, events, people – anything.

Have you ever fallen head over heels in love and then later realized it really wasn't love?

Can you describe someone who loves to be in love?

Do you know a Knight of Cups personality?

Queen of Cups

Empathic, emotional. Decisions based only on feelings. Kindly, loving, compassionate, generous and sweet natured. Loves babies and young children. A good listener and will emotionally support anyone in need.

How do you feel when you look at the Queen of Cups?

Do you see the Queen of Cups as positive, negative or neutral? Why?

What if the Queen of Cups is reversed?

A detailed description in your own words helps you to really feel the energy of a card. Write down a description of the Queen of Cups. Try to include every detail.

Make a list of keywords and phrases that help you to understand the Queen of Cups.

Thinking about your day, how did the Queen of Cups manifest itself? This can be about your emotions, memories, events, people – anything.

Describe how someone has helped you without any expectation of repayment.

How did this act make you feel?

Is it possible to help someone out of their negativity without becoming caught up in their pain?

Do you know a Queen of Cups?

King of Cups

Sincere, kindly and wise, he is a good mediator and diplomat. Open hearted but introverted. Appears weak and ineffective to some people although he usually isn't – he's merely keeping his own counsel until the time is right to speak.

____

____

____

How do you feel when you look at the King of Cups?

____

____

Do you see the King of Cups as positive, negative or neutral? Why?

____

____

____

What if the King of Cups is reversed?

____

____

A detailed description in your own words helps you to really feel the energy of a card. Write down a description of the King of Cups. Try to include every detail.

Make a list of keywords and phrases that help you to understand the King of Cups.

Thinking about your day, how did the King of Cups manifest itself? This can be about your emotions, memories, events, people – anything.

Can you identify any time when listening rather than speaking would be the wisest choice?

Who in your life provides a safe haven for you?

Who can you say anything to, knowing that they will never betray your confidence?

Do you provide the same role to others? If yes or no, explain why.

Ace of Pentacles

A new project, job or other source of income. A gift or prize. Prosperity. Savings. Home improvement.

How do you feel when you look at the Ace of Pentacles?

Do you see the Ace of Pentacles as positive, negative or neutral? Why?

What if the Ace of Pentacles is reversed?

A detailed description in your own words helps you to really feel the energy of a card. Write down a description of the Ace of Pentacles. Try to include every detail.

Make a list of keywords and phrases that help you to understand the Ace of Pentacles.

Thinking about your day, how did the Ace of Pentacles manifest itself? This can be about your emotions, memories, events, people – anything.

Do you view the work you do as a privilege or is a heavy load to bear?

What is the best gift you have ever received? Why?

What is the best gift you have ever given yourself? Why?

Two of Pentacles

Financial planning and budgeting. More money going out than coming in. Feeling as though resources (time, money) are stretched. Waiting for results: medical tests, exams, etc.

How do you feel when you look at the Two of Pentacles?

Do you see the Two of Pentacles as positive, negative or neutral? Why?

What if the Two of Pentacles is reversed?

A detailed description in your own words helps you to really feel the energy of a card. Write down a description of the Two of Pentacles. Try to include every detail.

Make a list of keywords and phrases that help you to understand the Two of Pentacles.

Thinking about your day, how did the Two of Pentacles manifest itself? This can be about your emotions, memories, events, people – anything.

Do you find having a busy life is stressful or invigorating? Why?

Do you enjoy the challenge of juggling several tasks and commitments to others?

Do you sometimes wish you could slow your life down?

If yes, what obstacles prevent you doing so?

Three of Pentacles

Project nears completion. Working as a team. Your skills stand you in good stead. End of a minor life cycle.

How do you feel when you look at the Three of Pentacles?

Do you see the Three of Pentacles as positive, negative or neutral? Why?

What if the Three of Pentacles is reversed?

A detailed description in your own words helps you to really feel the energy of a card. Write down a description of the Three of Pentacles. Try to include every detail.

Make a list of keywords and phrases that help you to understand the Three of Pentacles.

Thinking about your day, how did the Three of Pentacles manifest itself? This can be about your emotions, memories, events, people – anything.

When was the last time you were satisfied by a job well done?

Do you feel that you work better alone or as part of a team?

Why?

What may be ending in your life right now?

Four of Pentacles

Stability, security, accumulation of money. Cautious. Fear of risk. Prefers own company. Protective of personal wealth.

____

____

____

How do you feel when you look at the Four of Pentacles?

____

____

____

Do you see Four of Pentacles as positive, negative or neutral? Why? What if the Four of Pentacles is reversed?

____

____

____

A detailed description in your own words helps you to really feel the energy of a card. Write down a description of the Four of Pentacles. Try to include every detail.

____

Make a list of keywords and phrases that help you to understand the Four of Pentacles.

Thinking about your day, how did the Four of Pentacles manifest itself? This can be about your emotions, memories, events, people – anything.

The Course in Miracles teaches that nothing real can be destroyed. If this is the case, what, in your opinion is actually real?

Do you use belongings (such as name brand clothing) to define who you are?

Do you set aside happiness for achievement in the hope that there's time for happiness later?

Five of Pentacles

Material challenges. Lack of money, lack of adequate accommodation. Hard times. Health problems. Bad time to agree any financial commitment.

How do you feel when you look at the Five of Pentacles?

Do you see the Five of Pentacles as positive, negative or neutral? Why?

What if the Five of Pentacles is reversed?

A detailed description in your own words helps you to really feel the energy of a card. Write down a description of the Five of Pentacles. Try to include every detail.

Make a list of keywords and phrases that help you to understand the Five of Pentacles.

Thinking about your day, how did the Five of Pentacles manifest itself? This can be about your emotions, memories, events, people – anything.

As mentioned before, the Course in Miracles teaches that nothing real can be destroyed.

If you found yourself standing on the pavement with your family, having lost all your personal belongings and home, but your family was safe, would your emotional response be grief or relief? Why?

How would you help someone who has nothing?

Six of Pentacles

Sharing, giving, a debt repaid. Receiving, financial/material relief. Seeing others prosper while you remain in poverty.

____

____

____

How do you feel when you look at the Six of Pentacles?

____

____

____

Like the Five of Wands this is a 'three-way' card; which figure do you identify with?

____

____

____

Do you see the Six of Pentacles as positive, negative or neutral? Why? What if the Six of Pentacles is reversed?

____

A detailed description in your own words helps you to really feel the energy of a card. Write down a description of the Six of Pentacles. Try to include every detail.

Make a list of keywords and phrases that help you to understand the Six of Pentacles.

Thinking about your day, how did the Six of Pentacles manifest itself? This can be about your emotions, memories, events, people – anything.

Think about your life and where you stand on the average social scale.

Are you wealthy?

Do you feel the rich work for their money or does it come easily to them?

Is having material wealth often a question of luck or inheritance?

Which would you rather have, time or money?

Why?

What are your feelings about wealth?

Seven of Pentacles

Material wealth doesn't equal happiness. Appearances indicate satisfaction but life lacks purpose. Reassessment of priorities. Boredom. Loss of motivation.

How do you feel when you look at the Seven of Pentacles?

Do you see the Seven of Pentacles as positive, negative or neutral? Why?

What if the Seven of Pentacles is reversed?

A detailed description in your own words helps you to really feel the energy of a card. Write down a description of the Seven of Pentacles. Try to include every detail.

Make a list of keywords and phrases that help you to understand the Seven of Pentacles.

Thinking about your day, how did the Seven of Pentacles manifest itself? This can be about your emotions, memories, events, people – anything.

If your job is unfulfilling now, what keeps you there?

What action might you take if you become bored with your work or your life in general?

How would this action benefit you?

Eight of Pentacles

Honing existing talents, learning new skills. Change of profession. Doing something you love. Feeling fulfilled in your work. Taking up a new hobby. Working with your hands. Running a business.

How do you feel when you look at the Eight of Pentacles?

Do you see the Eight of Pentacles as positive, negative or neutral? Why?

What if the Eight of Pentacles is reversed?

A detailed description in your own words helps you to really feel the energy of a card. Write down a description of the Eight of Pentacles. Try to include every detail.

Make a list of keywords and phrases that help you to understand the Eight of Pentacles.

Thinking about your day, how did the Eight of Pentacles manifest itself? This can be about your emotions, memories, events, people – anything.

What puts you in a place of total focus and absorption?

Do you ever feel like that in your job?

If you could spend all day working or playing at one thing, what would it be?

Why?

Nine of Pentacles

Financial independence. Fulfilment. Contented with life achievements so far. May indicate a career break due to pregnancy. Singledom.

How do you feel when you look at the Nine of Pentacles?

Do you see the Nine of Pentacles as positive, negative or neutral? Why?

What if the Nine of Pentacles is reversed?

A detailed description in your own words helps you to really feel the energy of a card. Write down a description of the Nine of Pentacles. Try to include every detail.

Make a list of keywords and phrases that help you to understand the Nine of Pentacles.

Thinking about your day, how did the Nine of Pentacles manifest itself? This can be about your emotions, memories, events, people – anything.

Imagine you are the woman in the card image (Nine of Pentacles) – would you feel contented or bored?

Why?

Imagine having no pressure in your daily life.

How would your life be different than it is now?

Ten of Pentacles

Traditional family values. Legacy. Inheritance. An established family business. Paperwork all in order. Provisions made for future contingencies. A gathering together of family generations.

How do you feel when you look at the Ten of Pentacles?

Do you see the Ten of Pentacles as positive, negative or neutral? Why? What if the Ten of Pentacles is reversed?

A detailed description in your own words helps you to really feel the energy of a card.

Write down a description of the Ten of Pentacles. Try to include every detail.

Make a list of keywords and phrases that help you to understand the Ten of Pentacles.

Thinking about your day, how did the Ten of Pentacles manifest itself? This can be about your emotions, memories, events, people – anything.

Do you come from a family with strong ties and values?

Are those qualities important to you?

Do you think they will matter more as you grow older?

Why?

Page of Pentacles

Explorer, academic, scientist, student. Thirst for knowledge. Love of reading. Animal lover. A message delivered by mail or similar means, often regarding financial or property matters.

How do you feel when you look at the Page of Pentacles?

Do you see the Page of Pentacles as positive, negative or neutral? Why? What if the Page of Pentacles is reversed?

A detailed description in your own words helps you to really feel the energy of a card.

Write down a description of the Page of Pentacles. Try to include every detail.

Make a list of keywords and phrases that help you to understand the Page of Pentacles.

Thinking about your day, how did the Page of Pentacles manifest itself? This can be about your emotions, memories, events, people – anything.

What are you curious about? Make a list.

Knight of Pentacles

Trustworthy and reliable worker. "Still waters run deep". Not keen on sharing feelings. Hidden passion.

How do you feel when you look at the Knight of Pentacles?

Do you see the Knight of Pentacles as positive, negative or neutral? Why?

What if the Knight of Pentacles is reversed?

A detailed description in your own words helps you to really feel the energy of a card. Write down a description of the Knight of Pentacles. Try to include every detail.

Make a list of keywords and phrases that help you to understand the Knight of Pentacles.

Thinking about your day, how did the Knight of Pentacles manifest itself? This can be about your emotions, memories, events, people – anything.

Do you find the Knight of Pentacles to be personality fascinating?

Why or why not?

Do you know a Knight of Pentacles?

Compare him to the Knight of Pentacles on this card as you imagine him to be.

Queen of Pentacles

Practical, pragmatic, home-loving, creative, hard working. Encourages others to help themselves. A doer rather than a listener. Prefers to find her own way of doing things.

How do you feel when you look at the Queen of Pentacles?

Do you see the Queen of Pentacles as positive, negative or neutral? Why?

What if the Queen of Pentacles is reversed?

A detailed description in your own words helps you to really feel the energy of a card. Write down a description of the Queen of Pentacles. Try to include every detail.

Make a list of keywords and phrases that help you to understand the Queen of Pentacles.

Thinking about your day, how did the Queen of Pentacles manifest itself? This can be about your emotions, memories, events, people – anything.

The Queen of Pentacles is never bored; she always has some project on the go.

In what ways are you like (or not like) this queen?

What are your favorite hobbies, things to do, vacation spots – in other words, what are fun things you enjoy doing?

Why?

King of Pentacles

He is a self-made man, one who enjoys the fruits of his labor. May have issues with adult children; expecting them to do things the right way (as in his way). He adores his grandchildren and great grandchildren.

____

____

____

How do you feel when you look at the King of Pentacles?

____

____

____

Do you see the King of Pentacles as positive, negative or neutral? Why?

____

____

____

What if the King of Pentacles is reversed?

A detailed description in your own words helps you to really feel the energy of a card. Write down a description of the King of Pentacles. Try to include every detail.

Make a list of keywords and phrases that help you to understand the King of Pentacles.

Thinking about your day, how did the King of Pentacles manifest itself? This can be about your emotions, memories, events, people – anything.

The King of Pentacles believes that because his method of doing things worked well for him, this is the way everyone should then do the same process.

Do you agree?

Why or why not?

Do you know a King of Pentacles type?

Describe him or her?

Ace of Swords

Sudden understanding, clarity of thought, new methods of communication. Efficiency. The truth revealed; the curtain is pulled back. A new way of perceiving the world.

How do you feel when you look at the Ace of Swords?

Do you see the Ace of Swords as positive, negative or neutral? Why?

What if the Ace of Swords is reversed?

A detailed description in your own words helps you to really feel the energy of a card. Write down a description of the Ace of Swords. Try to include every detail.

Make a list of keywords and phrases that help you to understand the Ace of Swords.

Thinking about your day, how did the Ace of Swords manifest itself? This can be about your emotions, memories, events, people – anything.

The mindset of the Ace of Swords is – clarity, simplicity and singleness. Having these attributes gives our lives joy and also power.

Do you agree with the mindset of the Ace of Swords?

Why or why not?

Do you see the power in clarity?

What area(s) in your life are lacking in clarity? Why?

Two of Swords

The Two of Swords indicates preventing oneself from seeing the truth, refusing to engage, reluctance to make a decision. Self-protection.

How do you feel when you look at the Two of Swords?

Do you see the Two of Swords as positive, negative or neutral? Why?

What if the Two of Swords is reversed?

A detailed description in your own words helps you to really feel the energy of a card. Write down a description of the Two of Swords. Try to include every detail.

Make a list of keywords and phrases that help you to understand the Two of Swords.

Thinking about your day, how did the Two of Swords manifest itself? This can be about your emotions, memories, events, people – anything.

Have you ever refused to face up to something for fear of starting an argument?

Briefly describe the situation that came to mind.

How did you feel?

If you haven't been in a situation like this, could you imagine ever doing so? If so, how do you think you would act?

Three of Swords

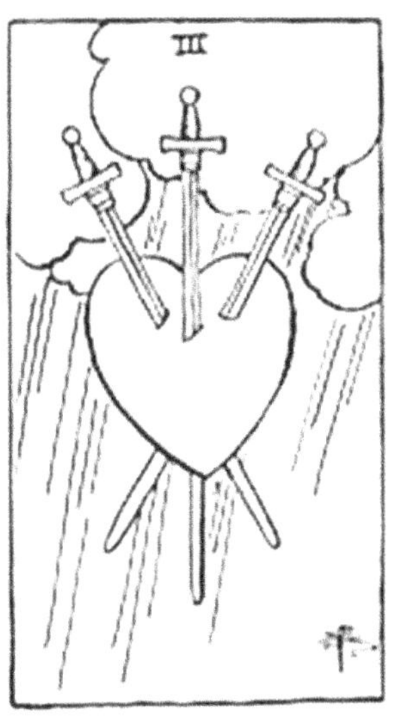

Communication difficulties. Mixed messages; tangled wires. Separation, misunderstanding. Medical procedures.

____

____

____

How do you feel when you look at the Three of Swords?

____

____

____

Do you see the Three of Swords as positive, negative or neutral? Why? What if the Three of Swords is reversed?

____

____

____

A detailed description in your own words helps you to really feel the energy of a card.

Write down a description of the Three of Swords. Try to include every detail.

Make a list of keywords and phrases that help you to understand the Three of Swords.

Thinking about your day, how did the Three of Swords manifest itself? This can be about your emotions, memories, events, people – anything.

The Three of Swords card is often thought to mean heartbreak.

Do you think heartbreak is a misunderstanding?

Explore how heartbreak might ensue from a breakdown in communication?

Four of Swords

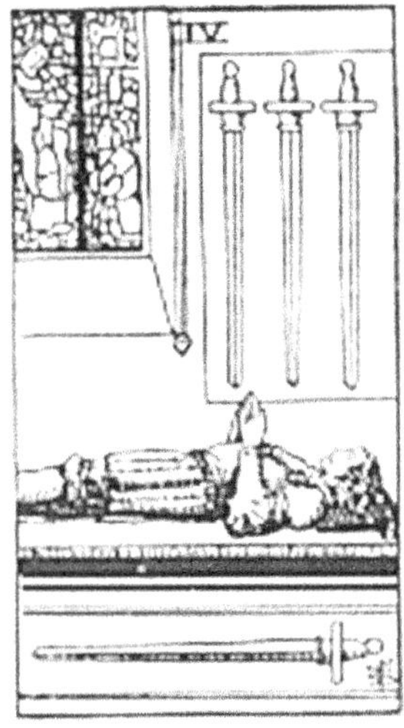

Illness resulting in a forced rest or down time. Taking time for oneself out of necessity.

____

____

____

How do you feel when you look at the Four of Swords?

____

____

____

Do you see the Four of Swords as positive, negative or neutral? Why?

____

____

____

What if the Four of Swords is reversed?

____

A detailed description in your own words helps you to really feel the energy of a card. Write down a description of the Four of Swords. Try to include every detail.

Make a list of keywords and phrases that help you to understand the Four of Swords.

Thinking about your day, how did the Four of Swords manifest itself? This can be about your emotions, memories, events, people – anything.

Do you have stress in your life?

What stresses you the most?

Describe how you deal with stress.

Five of Swords

Deceit, bullying, defeat. Disengagement. Hollow victory. Gain at the expense of others.

How do you feel when you look at the Five of Swords?

Which figure do you identify with? The victor in the foreground, the person walking away in the middle ground or the defeated one in the background?

Why?

Do you see the Five of Swords as positive, negative or neutral?

Why?

What if the Five of Swords is reversed?

A detailed description in your own words helps you to really feel the energy of a card. Write down a description of the Five of Swords. Try to include every detail.

Make a list of keywords and phrases that help you to understand the Five of Swords.

Thinking about your day, how did the Five of Swords manifest itself? This can be about your emotions, memories, events, people – anything.

Have you ever been bullied?

How did it make you feel?

Did you ever bully someone else?

How did it make you feel?

Six of Swords

Consistent progress in a calm and steady manner. Learning from life's lessons and moving on, calmly and focused. Using guidance from within oneself.

How do you feel when you look at the Six of Swords?

Are you the person moving the boat or the passenger?

Where are you headed?

Do you see the Six of Swords as positive, negative or neutral? Why?

What if the Six of Swords is reversed?

A detailed description in your own words helps you to really feel the energy of a card. Write down a description of the Six of Swords. Try to include every detail.

Make a list of keywords and phrases that help you to understand the Six of Swords.

Thinking about your day, how did the Six of Swords manifest itself? This can be about your emotions, memories, events, people – anything.

Have you noticed that once you stop thinking about something bad that has happened to you, you move forward at a much faster pace?

Why do you think this happens?

How do you feel when you dwell on past things that have hurt you?

Why do you think this is?

Seven of Swords

This card represents deception, theft, a sneaky attitude. The finding of Something lost be it a material item or self-esteem, self confidence or peace of mind.

____

____

____

How do you feel when you look at the Seven of Swords?

____

____

____

Do you think he a thief or do think that the swords belong to him?

____

____

____

Why?

Do you see the Seven of Swords as positive, negative or neutral? Why?

What if the Seven of Swords is reversed?

A detailed description in your own words helps you to really feel the energy of a card. Write down a description of the Seven of Swords. Try to include every detail.

Make a list of keywords and phrases that help you to understand the Seven of Swords.

Thinking about your day, how did the Seven of Swords manifest itself? This can be about your emotions, memories, events, people – anything.

Do you think that sometimes we have to act like thieves for a higher cause?

Do you think that sort of action is justified?

Describe the last time you (or someone you are close to) were a victim of theft.

How did it make you (or them) feel?

Eight of Swords

This card represents being backed in a corner or trapped.

Surrounded by problems of your own doing. Lacking in power and also lacking in confidence. Frozen in place, unable to move.

A fear of the future.

How do you feel when you look at the Eight of Swords?

Do you see the Eight of Swords as positive, negative or neutral? Why?

What if the Eight of Swords is reversed?

A detailed description in your own words helps you to really feel the energy of a card. Write down a description of the Eight of Swords. Try to include every detail.

Make a list of keywords and phrases that help you to understand the Eight of Swords.

Thinking about your day, how did the Eight of Swords manifest itself? This can be about your emotions, memories, events, people – anything.

Have you ever felt paralyzed by fear?

Describe the situation and how it made you feel.

How did you overcome this feeling?

Nine of Swords

This card represents anxiety, nightmares, worry, fear.

Being unable to see a solution.

How do you feel when you look at the Nine of Swords?

Do you see the Nine of Swords as positive, negative or neutral? Why?

What if the Nine of Swords is reversed?

A detailed description in your own words helps you to really feel the energy of a card. Write down a description of the Nine of Swords. Try to include every detail.

Make a list of keywords and phrases that help you to understand the Nine of Swords.

Thinking about your day, how did the Nine of Swords manifest itself?

Do you have sleepless nights due to anxiety?

When you look back, what percentage of what you are anxious about comes into being?

Do you consider worrying to be a productive activity?

Why or why not?

Ten of Swords

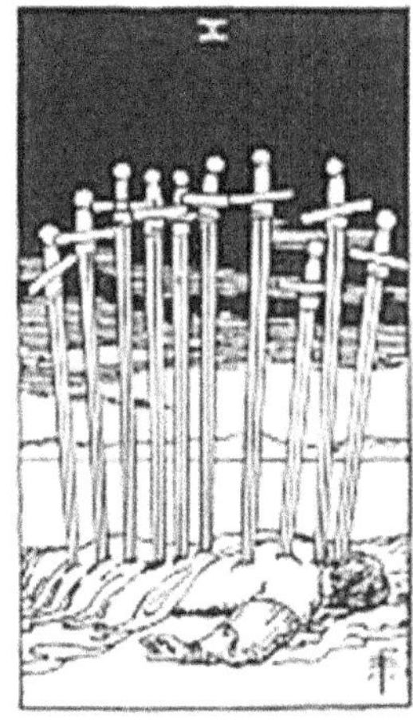

This card represents the end of a cycle. Something long established is now finished. A new beginning is coming. Light at the end of the tunnel. This card can indicate a death when in combination with other cards.

How do you feel when you look at the Ten of Swords?

Do you see the Ten of Swords as positive, negative or neutral? Why?

What if the Ten of Swords is reversed?

A detailed description in your own words helps you to really feel the energy of a card. Write down a description of the Ten of Swords. Try to include every detail.

Make a list of keywords and phrases that help you to understand the Ten of Swords.

Thinking about your day, how did the Ten of Swords manifest itself? This can be about your emotions, memories, events, people – anything.

When your elderly or ill dog passes away after living a rewarding and good life, the best compliment you can give him or her it to get yourself another dog. Be it a puppy or older.

Do you agree?

Why or why not?

When something ends do you look forward to a new beginning?

Why or why not?

Page of Swords

Explorer of thought and philosophy. Always asking questions. Transformation of ideas into reality. Quick thinker, good communicator, excellent debater. A message delivered swiftly

How do you feel when you look at the Page of Swords?

Do you see the Page of Swords as positive, negative or neutral? Why? What if the Page of Swords is reversed?

A detailed description in your own words helps you to really feel the energy of a card. Write down a description of the Page of Swords. Try to include every detail.

Make a list of keywords and phrases that help you to understand the Page of Swords.

Thinking about your day, how did the Page of Swords manifest itself? This can be about your emotions, memories, events, people – anything.

What kinds of profession would attract a Page of Swords?

What would be his or her typical free-time activities?

If the Page of Swords was real person, describe his/her personality.

Do you know a Page of Swords?

Describe him or her.

Knight of Swords

Fights for a cause. Single-minded, laser-focused, determined, highly intelligent. Impatient. Tendency to be critical of others.

How do you feel when you look at the Knight of Swords?

Do you see the Knight of Swords as positive, negative or neutral? Why?

What if the Knight of Swords is reversed?

A detailed description in your own words helps you to really feel the energy of a card. Write down a description of the Knight of Swords. Try to include every detail.

Make a list of keywords and phrases that help you to understand the Knight of Swords.

Thinking about your day, how did the Knight of Swords manifest itself? This can be about your emotions, memories, events, people – anything.

What does the Knight of Swords think about when he's not on a mission?

List some of his qualities.

Would he make a good life partner?

Why or why not?

Queen of Swords

Seeker of truth. Intellectual, intelligent, incisive. Straight talker. Highly motivated, professional and efficient. Witty and flirty if she thinks it's necessary. Will take advice from others if she respects their opinion. Can be hard-hearted.

How do you feel when you look at the Queen of Swords?

Do you see the Queen of Swords as positive, negative or neutral? Why?

What if the Queen of Swords is reversed?

A detailed description in your own words helps you to really feel the energy of a card. Write down a description of the Queen of Swords. Try to include every detail.

Make a list of keywords and phrases that help you to understand the Queen of Swords.

Thinking about your day, how did the Queen of Swords manifest itself? This can be about your emotions, memories, events, people – anything.

How and when might the Queen of Swords show a more vulnerable side?

Have you ever known a Queen of Swords?

Did you like her? Describe her personality.

King of Swords

Authoritarian. Takes responsibility, good communicator, logical, clear thinker, commands respect. Usually at the top of his profession (lawyer, surgeon, writer, etc.).

____

____

____

How do you feel when you look at the King of Swords?

____

____

____

Do you see the King of Swords as positive, negative or neutral? Why?

____

____

____

What if the King of Swords is reversed?

____

A detailed description in your own words helps you to really feel the energy of a card. Write down a description of the King of Swords. Try to include every detail.

Make a list of keywords and phrases that help you to understand the King of Swords.

Thinking about your day, how did the King of Swords manifest itself? This can be about your emotions, memories, events, people – anything.

Imagine if the King of Swords had been married for many years and then lost his wife.

How would he act?

How would he cope?

Write a few paragraphs about him dealing with life on his own.

Congratulations

You've worked your way one by one through the Rider-Waite tarot card deck.

This is NOT a small accomplishment.

Give yourself a lot of credit for accomplishing this large project.

Please feel free to go back as often as you wish to review the material you have learned. You may find your previous answers to questions change as time passes. This is quite often the case and just indicates how you yourself are growing and changing.

Before we wrap up, we have selected a few popular Tarot card spreads so you can see the layouts and have a guide to use when practicing.

Tarot Card Spreads

Card readers and those they read for often wonder what card spreads are the most valuable and also most common.

We'll walk through 6 common, easy to use, valuable card spreads.

You may find you prefer one spread over all the others. You may want to custom tailor the spread you will use based on the person you are doing the reading for.

The card spreads are not listed in any particular order.

Each spread also has a basic script.

This will provide some insight regarding what to say as you lay each card down

The True Love Spread

For the most part, most everyone wants to know what direction their love life is headed, what will happen and if they will be happy.

This spread is very useful to evaluate your physical, emotional, mental and spiritual connections with your partner.

This is a six-card spread.

#1– This card represents you. It signifies what you currently feel about your relationship, your approach, and your outlook.

#2– The second card represent your partner. It also represents his current emotions towards you, his attitude, and expectations about your relationship.

#3– This is a connection card. What are the characteristics that you have in common binding you together?

#4– This indicates the strength of your relationship. What are the qualities that keep your relationship?

#5– This denotes the weakness of your relationship. What are the things you both need to improve?

#6– This final card is your true love card. It interprets what needs to be addressed. Is your relationship going to be successful? If there is a threat, what must be done?

The Success Spread

The success spread an excellent spread to use when you are facing an obstacle or challenge and do not know how to approach it.

This spread helps you to better understand the true nature of the obstacle you face, as well as helping you to identify what skills and resources you have at your disposal to not just face, but also overcome these obstacles!

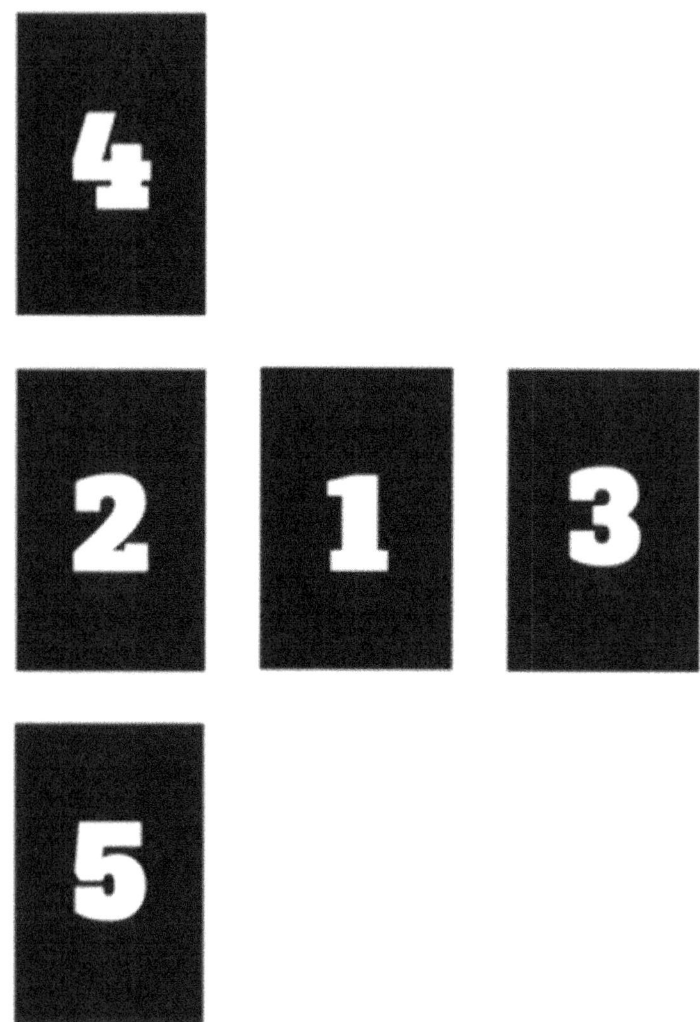

#1– This card signifies your major concern or obstacle.

#2– This card talks about your current challenges and complications.

#3– This card reveals the hidden factors that you need to know affecting your current situation.

#4– This card represents new ideas, people, or things that can help you grow further.

#5– This is the indicator of what you need to do to be successful or what you should avoid do to avoid failure.

The Celtic Cross Spread

Despite its complexity, the "Celtic Cross" is a spread that has been in used for many, many years. It is a personal favorite of many who read tarot cards.

In its complexity is the true beauty of this spread.

I find this spread to be the most helpful in complicated situations, because it's versatile and its positions deliver vast amount of information that can be read in several ways depending on the combinations.

It points to issues that are of the client's own making, but also shows what outside influences are at play.

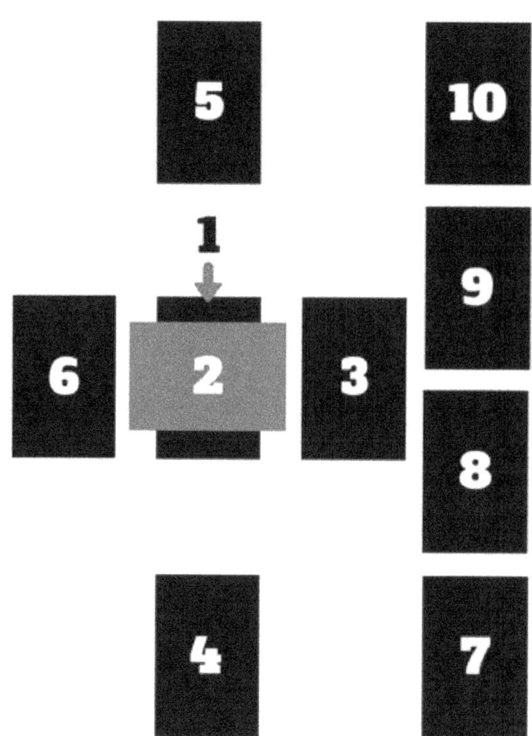

#1– It presents your current situation.

#2– This across card will either tell you what is helping you or what is holding you back.

#3– It tackles your subconscious influences. What does your heart truly desire that you are unaware of? These influences you do not know have powerful effect in your everyday life.

#4 –This is your past card. What past events or issues are bugging your life until now? Bad past may have an adverse effect in your current situation that you probably need to let go real soon, and good past must be acknowledged as your life inspiration.

#5– This card deals with your conscious desires. What are your objectives and goals that are of extreme value to you right now? This is where you should place your strongest energy. Depending on the card, it may also signify how you should use that energy.

#6 –This is your headlight. Where are you going? What path are you tracing? If the card says there is a negative energy on your way, what can you do to avoid it? How will you redirect your life to a better track?

#7– This card is your attitude. It represents your actions, thoughts, and ideals.

#8– This is an energy card. What kind of energy do you get from the people surrounding you and your environment? Are they helpful?

#9– This is a revelation card. It signifies the things that you should know and be aware of in your current situation. Something you should never neglect.

#10 –This is your final card, and it means your final outcome. Based on your current energies, this will have a strong connection with your #5 card. What does it say? Are the energies complementing or conflicting each other?

The Spiritual Guidance Spread

The Spiritual Guidance spread is used situationally during times when you are faced with obstacles or challenges of a spiritual nature, usually related to your own growth or development.

This spread is designed to give you a broader perspective and includes information to help you along your spiritual path and important life lessons.

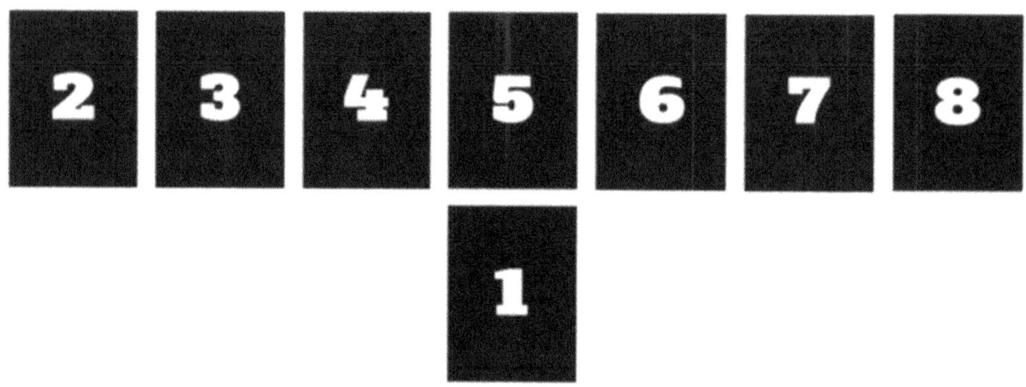

#1 –This is your primary concern, question, or issue.

#2 –This card interprets your motivation for your quest for guidance.

#3 –This card identifies the areas in your life you are anxious or upset about.

#4 –This card signifies the events in your current situation that you are unaware of.

#5 –This is your advice card. It will provide you knowledge on what you should do or not do to overcome your apprehensions.

#6 –This card will tell you the best way to proceed from your worries and what you should do to keep moving.

#7 –This card tells you how to move forward with a positive light.

#8 –Finally, this card wraps up the possible results you will get if you are able to follow the guide light successfully.

The Career Path Spread

If you're an employee who feels like you have remained stagnant, stuck in a rut for years, vying to be promoted, but to no gain, this spread is for you.

It is a great spread that will help you to understand any obstacles you may be facing in your professional life and suggest strategies to on how to deal with these issues.

Alternatively, if you are unhappy with your current career choice, this is the spread to use to suggest alternative paths based on your personal strengths.

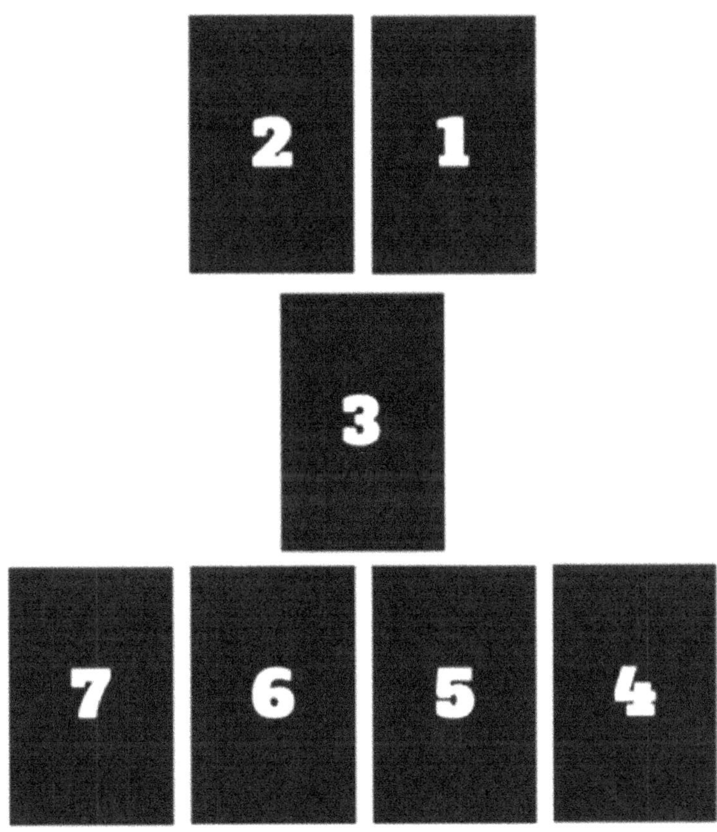

#1– This card interprets the answer to the question: Is your current job your ideal job?

#2– This card signifies what actions must be taken to further your career.

#3– This card reveals the aspects in your career life that you can no longer alter.

#4– This card shows your level of performance in your current job. Are you exerting enough effort to get to the top or even to accelerate?

#5– The fifth card tells you the things that you need to change and improve.

#6– This answers the question: Is there a past event in your career life that is affecting your current work status?

#7– This final card interprets the result that you must anticipate if you follow the spread promptly.

The Three Card Spread

Do not let the incredible simplicity of this spread deceive you.

This is one of the most powerful Tarot card spreads.

It is the quickest way to get answers and if I don't have the time needed to do a different spread, this one cuts to the chase.

It is wonderfully helpful in lasering in on the energy (past, present and future) surrounding your question.

The Three Card Spread is very different in comparison to the other spreads that we've discussed.

There is not a fixed purpose to each card, instead it is incredibly flexible depending upon the question being asked.

Here are the variations -

#1– Past/Present/Future

#2– What helps you/What hinders you/What are your realized and unrealized potentials

#3– Current situation/Challenges/Guidance

#4– 1 What you think/What you feel/What you do

#5– You/Your partner/Your relationship

#6– Mind/Body/Spirit

I think now you will see, after looking at the options above, how incredibly flexible this spread can be.

Closing

Thank you for purchasing this workbook. We hope that you found it to be a helpful and valuable learning tool for mastering tarot cards.

Learning each card does take time and ideally this book has made each card come to life and feel like a friend.

Learning the various spreads won't happen overnight.

You may find one spread that you prefer but, I do suggest learning all of them so you can do the reading fluidly if for some reason a client prefers a different spread.

We publish the majority of our books in the 8 ½ x 11 sized format as like most people, we don't like squinting at tiny print and also like to have plenty of room to write.

We hope having a larger size workbook was beneficial.

www.ingramcontent.com/pod-product-compliance
Lightning Source LLC
Chambersburg PA
CBHW081213130726
47997CB00009B/2641